YOUR KNOWLEDGE HAS VALUE

Law, order, and democracy. The legal sphere of women in ancient Athens

Lisa Turan

Bibliographic information published by the German National Library:

The German National Library lists this publication in the National Bibliography; detailed bibliographic data are available on the Internet at http://dnb.dnb.de.

ISBN: 9783346919250
This book is also available as an ebook.

Print and binding: Books on Demand GmbH, Norderstedt, Germany
Printed on acid-free paper from responsible sources.

The present work has been carefully prepared. Nevertheless, authors and publishers do not incur liability for the correctness of information, notes, links and advice as well as any printing errors.

GRIN web shop: https://www.grin.com/document/1379697

University of H.

Faculty of History

Everyday life in Athens (Proseminar)

"Law, order, and democracy: The legal sphere of women in ancient Athens"

27 January 2023

Lisa Turan

Main subject: Education (Sek. I/II)

1. Minor: English

2. Minor: History

Contents:

"Law, order, and democracy: The legal sphere of women in ancient Athens"

Around the 5th century BC, the people of ancient Athens pioneered the concept of *demo-kratia*, a system of self-governance that means power to the people in its original sense (Rhodes 3). Different from previous regimes, the establishment of democracy guaranteed direct political and legal access for free Athenian citizens despite wealth, property, or power relations (Kapparis 113).

Nevertheless, there is fierce controversy concerning the question of how democratic the Attic legal system was for the female population. Critics claim among others the arbitrariness of judgments, and the lack of legal education of most of Athens's population who was neither in the position to make proper decisions in court nor to revise verdicts (Burkhard 8), in addition to gender inequality with regards to the access to Athens's law system (Kapparis 1). Most strikingly is that previous work in this field focused predominantly on the scope of men within the justice system, while written pieces concerting female voices barely exist. Ultimately, this urges us to ask whether the Athenian justice system provided legal access for women and how they have been legally prosecuted at the time.

Accordingly, I begin my research paper by the attempt to analyze social and legal conventions for women within the male-dominated society of ancient Athens. I will then take into account the key mechanisms of the Athenian justice system to compare the legal accessibility for women in comparison to men. Consequently, I will discuss a controversial case according to the speech of Lysias named "To Antigenes, on the abortion" within which the plaintiff Antigenes accused his wife of homicide due to an induced abortion without his consent. By this, I try to identify the legal situation of the female as the perpetrator as well as a potential outcome to the case for her.

At this point, it is worth noting that the situation cannot be measured for all Athenian women equally. At the time of ancient Athens, there were serious differences between married and unmarried females (Kitto 56), as well as legal, social, and economic disparities (Kapparis 106). Moreover, female slaves were completely excluded from all legal actions (118). I follow from what I said and will mainly focus on free and married Athenian women due to the scope of the following research paper.

To cover the broad spectrum of the research field, I will evaluate the secondary literature of various scholars, among others Leonhard Burkhard, Gerhardt Thür, P. J. Rhodes, Laura Pepe, S. C. Todd, and Konstantinos Kapparis to discuss their theories and concepts.

1. LEGAL AND SOCIAL CONVENTIONS FOR ATHENIAN WOMEN

Historical research on antiquity distributes the assumption that women in ancient Athens lived under the rough domination of men, who seemingly excluded Athenian women from the legal system (Kapparis 1).

So far, evidence shows that gender relations in ancient Athens were in fact not equal. Indeed, women were legally and socially dependent on their closest male relative *kýrios*, a guardian, which was either their father, husband, or brother (Schmitz 101), and the life of men and women were divided (Katz 41) by gender into public and private spaces (Schnurr-Redford 14). Beyond, customs required men to frequently engage in the public life of the *polis*, Athens's city-state, while women spent most of their time within their households called *oikos* to manage family affairs (Schnurr-Redford 14). Females who worked outside their households even conveyed distrust and humility for their families (14).

One might argue that the above portrayal resembles a subordinate and homebound life for women who were apparently restricted to make independent or legal decisions. Despite we do not know how women perceived their lifestyles due to a lack of sources written by Athenian women, scholars argue that the picture of the Athenian woman living in an "oriental harem-slavery" (Katz 36) is in all likelihood inappropriate (Schmitz 101). To illustrate the problem, scholar Marilyn Katz claims this contemporary assumption to be a product of historians from the 18th century, who interpreted the subordinate Athenian women according to John Lock's thesis of "freedom and equality as a birthright" (Katz 39). Lock's thesis says that men are the owners of their bodies, and property, and are the only species that has legal rights in comparison to women who are subordinate to their husbands by nature (39). Katz concludes that many kinds of research were "significantly conditioned by the contemporary discussion on language, nationalism, and race" (42) which helps to explain why contemporary assumptions might not resemble the accurate historical reality of ancient Athens.

Applying to the above, H. D. F. Kitto appeals to differentiate the past from the present because the social conditions of ancient Athens cannot be compared to our modern understanding of liberty (48). He acknowledges that most of the Athenian women might have lived a life in oriental seclusion (55), but the primary source of concern is that the freedom of individuals is not self-evident, but a "local development" (49), which declares that Athenian women of their time might not have considered themselves as suppressed. In this regard, Kitto's perspective compels us to consider the legal role of Athenian women in the context of past social conventions.

As Katz and Kitto rightfully observed, it is important to keep in mind the social and legal conventions according to the times of ancient Athens. In this regard, I will infuse their ideas and try to reconsider contemporary perceptions about ancient Athenian womanhood with an impartial view, for which I will compare previous with modern research in order to detect their legal space within the Attic justice system. Appropriately, this question will be further investigated in the next section.

2. FEMALE ACCESS TO THE ATHENIAN JUSTICE SYSTEM

To evaluate the accessibility for women it is necessary to take the key components of Athens's justice system into account. The contributions of Gerhard Thür and Leonhard Burkhard in "Grosse Prozesse im antiken Athen." allow us factual insights into Athens's justice system, however addressing a rather male-focused perspective. As comparing approaches, I will therefore complement Thür and Burkhard's research with P. J. Rhodes's "Athenian Democracy" as well as the most recent publication of Konstantinos Kapparis named "Women in the Law Courts of Classical Athens".

As previously mentioned, the public and private spheres were separated by gender. From a holistic point of view, public access for the male population of Athens's democracy was enabled by an open assembly named ekklesia, supervised by 500 annually changing representatives of the council, the boule (Rhodes 3). Besides existed an elaborated justice system, of which the highest instance was the main trial, the dikasterion (Kapparis 111). The system was accessible through different stages – the lower layer was represented by the magistrates of the state as civil servants, who dealt with smaller delicts on behalf of the people (Thür 33). While Thür's approach observes the key mechanisms but lacks with regards to female access to the judiciary system, the circumstances gain a more accurate shape when Kapparis indicates the possibility for free women to equally submit requests, make complaints, or file for divorce without the consent of their *kýrios* at the magistrates of the state (Kapparis 107). On the contrary, slave women had no access to them at all (118).

More to the point, judicial processes belonged to the higher layer and were divided into public actions for communal affairs, and private actions for individual matters (Kapparis 124)). If citizens pitched a case, both sides had to go through pre-trial proceedings and sometimes the main trial (Thür 32). The general way was that the plaintiff informed the defendant about the accusation (33). When the accusation was accepted, the parties discussed the matter at a pre-trial named *anákrisis* (33). Finally, if the parties were not able to achieve an agreement, they needed to appear personally in the *dikasterion*, where the verdict was delivered by a jury (34). Kapparis acknowledges that women could not speak on their behalf and needed a *synegoros*, a legal representative, to get access to the trials (105), who have been a family member or friend of the litigant (114). However, he emphasizes that Athens's justice system performed in the sense of democracy, which means that it was not illegal for females to speak in front of the court, but rather a social custom of the times (111).

This might blend into the fact that women had legal access to trials, but not without representation (Kapparis 111). However notable is that proper rhetoric had an enormous impact on the outcome of the verdict (Burkhard 164). The centrality of this point can be seen in the point that it was also common for Athenian men to seek help from speechwriters or advocates disregarding gender (Kapparis 115). Consequently, speechwriters were professionals in the disciplines of writing, psychology, and the comprehension of law (113) that were apparently useful for male and female defendants likewise. Moreover, as most of the trial processes were put into writing (Thür 38), the argument can be strengthened by the assumption that most Athenian women might have been illiterate (Kitto 54), and their representation would have been more of an advantage than a disadvantage. In this light, my argument is that we cannot per se talk about the exclusion of women according to the social customs of their time.

Thus, a counterexample to the above is the accessibility of positions within the jury. Only debtless, male Athenian citizens at the age of 30 were able to apply for a job at the court's jury (Burkhard 163) for which they were chosen by lottery (Rhodes 4). Each jury consisted of 201 to 2501 men, depending on the value in dispute (Thür 31). The lawsuit was accessible to spectators (Burkhard 164). We cannot say for sure, however, it is very likely, women did not participate in these sorts of public events due to contemporary conventions. In terms of the main trials, data shows that it started with the libel reading, including witness statements (Thür 46). According to Kapparis, women could have participated in witness interviews equally to men (109). After the court speeches, the jury directly voted on behalf of one party (Thür 47), irreversible by a higher instance (37). Finally, Kapparis emphasizes in his records that if a grown-up woman mistreated the law, she "was always responsible for her actions before the law" (115) and had to face the consequences of her incorrect behavior equally to men and was not protected by the oikos to bypass a verdict (115).

It would not be a simplification to say that all of the above contributions provide a sober display of the legal apparatus of ancient Athens. Objectively, all authors are children of their time and research in this regard, however, it can be argued that the engagement of women was not further meaningful for Thür and Burkhard's analysis. Nevertheless, Kapparis demonstrated that the Athenian justice system acted in the name of democracy "regardless of gender or social status" (115) and proved that it was no one-sided mechanism of social control, as Thür concluded (49), but just according to the social customs of antiquity. The next step will be to find out how the Athenian law sentenced women based on a precarious law case.

3. DISCUSSION: "TO ANTIGENES, ON THE ABORTION"

Integrally combined with the above, I proved that there have been certain spheres for women within the Athenian legal system, however, constrained in comparison to men. Eventually, I will return to the key question of this paper and examine how women might have been prosecuted in court. In this regard, I will focus on the example of abortion and discuss speech fragments of Lysias' speeches named "*To Antigenes, on the abortion*" revolving around the questions of the situation of the female in charge and the legal consequences she might have had to face.

The speech has been analyzed by various scholars ever since. Konstantinos Kapparis refers to the circumstances as "an extraordinary and truly intriguing case, which seemingly pushed the boundaries of Athenian legal procedure with arguments which were more akin to philosophy and medicine than Athenian homicide law" (23). What we know today is an Athenian man called Antigenes sued his unknown wife for homicide because she caused an abortion and prevented Antigenes from fatherhood (25), which makes the case unique and difficult likewise.

The problem with the oration is that parts of the content only survived through other ancient scholars, among others Theon, Sopater, or Hippocrates, who referenced *"On the Abortion"* within their discussions. This means that it is very difficult to reconcile the circumstances of the event properly (Todd 238). In addition, there is uncertainty about whether the title of the speech has been translated correctly, which is important to understand whether Antigenes was the prosecutor or defendant (240). In fact, there are multiple theories about the relations between the participants. Scholar S. C. Todd argues that according to the references within the fragments, it is very likely that Antigenes accused his wife due to the abortion because she acted without his consent against his will and divorced her after her deed, however, he emphasizes that we cannot know for sure, and should keep in mind that the situation remains speculative (240). Due to the extent of this paper, I will concentrate on the above-introduced assumption to analyze her legal spheres.

In a similar fashion, there is further speculation concerning the speech's authenticity because it cannot be proved with certainty whether Lysias is truly the author of the piece and if he wrote the speech for a law court or just as an exercise for rhetoric students (Todd 239). Todd disagrees with the latter idea due to the very detailed information the author provides, which is obviously too explicit for a rhetorical exercise (239). However, to discuss the above case, it might primarily be important to take the fragments into account. Essentially, I will provide five of the surviving fragments of the speech to discuss their content:

1. Lys. fr. 20b (ed. Carey 2007): "Several disputable arguments have already been put forward by the orators…as in the speech of Lysias 'On the abortion' … In that speech, the question is whether what is carried in the womb is a human being and whether women can have abortions without fear of a penalty. Some people claim that these speeches were not written by Lysias, but it would be beneficial for young people to read these too for the sake of exercise."

2. Lys. fr. 20d (ed. Carey 2007): "Lysias is dealing with a medical question, which he paradoxically converts into a rhetorical subject in the speech 'On the abortion', where Antigenes is accusing his wife of homicide because she had an induced abortion; he maintains that she had an abortion and prevented him from being called the father of the child."

3. Lys. fr. 20c (ed. Carey 2007): "There are also medical and philosophical questions, an example of a medical question is the one discussed by Lysias, namely whether a man who made a woman have an abortion has committed murder, for it is necessary to know if it (the fetus) was a living being before it was born. And this is a matter pertinent to medicine and natural philosophy."

4. Lys. fr. 20a (ed. Carey 2007): "For example, Lysias in the speech 'On the abortion' where the person responsible is on trial for murder goes to great lengths to prove that the fetus (brephos) is a living being and says everywhere 'as the doctors and the midwives have stated'."

5. Hip. Epid. 2,2,19 (ed. Carey 2007): "The wife of Antigenes, the only living near Nichomachos' place, produced a fetus which was fleshy, with the major organs already shaped, about four fingers long, but without bones, and then round and thick. Before labor she became asthmatic, then during labor, some pus came out, as if from a boil."

(Translation Kapparis 2021, p. 23-25)

Regardless of the doubts about Lysias as the actual author of the speech, which we already discussed beforehand, the content of the fragments is closely related. Therefore, in order to detect the legal situation for the defendant woman, several questions need to be clarified. To find answers to the above-stated questions, it is necessary to identify how abortion has been socially perceived in ancient Athens. To start, I will focus on the question of whether the fetus had been considered a human being in order to detect if the accusation of homicide was justified and what legal consequences could have occurred for her.

As the topic is very complex, there are different ways of argumentation. From a medical perspective, evidence shows that the Oath of Hippocrates (460-380 B.C.) forbade induced abortions for women (Korkuta 116). They devoted themselves to the principles of Pythagoras (116) and considered a fetus as a human being since its organs had developed (117). However, there was no legal punishment for them if they acted against the Oath (116).

Different from the above was the philosophical interpretation of abortion. According to Plato, the ideal pregnancy age for women was close to our modern understanding of between twenty and forty (Todd 236). He consented to abortion when the mother-to-be was above that age, but only if the abortion was practiced by midwives (236). Likewise, he and his companion Aristotle both agreed that Athens's population should stay within the limits of 5040 citizens and permitted abortion if the number was about to surpass (Korkuta 117). Aristotle further mentioned that abortion was only acceptable as long as the fetus had not developed body parts (Todd 236). Different from disabled babies, he forbade to exposure healthy babies after birth (236). Noteworthy, women who aborted or miscarried a fetus were not allowed to visit holy places anymore from a religious point of view (Pepe 40).

As displayed above, there have been different opinions on abortion in ancient Athens, all exclusively provided by men without the consideration of female interests. Even if the social conventions only allowed abortion in certain circumstances, at least from a legal perspective, no law in ancient Athens prohibited abortion (Kapparis 25), which answers the above question insofar as to say that there was on the one side no legal punishment for women who seek medical help to end a pregnancy, on the other side no legal penalty for doctors and midwives if they acted against the Hippocratic Oath. At the same time, scholar Laura Pepe argues that a law against prohibition did not exist simply because there was no interference from the state needed (Pepe 59). The decision of whether to accept or abandon a child from or into the oikos was always the man's duty, hence such a law was unnecessary because it was common sense for women to have the husband's consent for abortion (43).

If Pepe's assumption is particularly true, this raises the question about the legal status of the woman in charge and whether Antigenes was still married to the woman during the trial. As Todd notes, the fragmentary transmission makes it difficult to find out about the exact circumstances for sure, which means that multiple options are possible (249). For brevity, I will not discuss all variations in detail and focus on whether Antigenes and his wife were married or divorced. By the fact that the woman in charge was represented by her adult son, likely, she was previously married to another husband (the father of her son) and at the time of the trial divorced from Antigenes, which means that she might not have legally belonged to Antigenes oikos anymore, but under the protection of her son as her next kyrios (Todd 242).

From a distant point of view, we have already clarified that abortion is a private matter, and the male head of the oikos decides about the abortion or eventual penalty for his wife. Even in the case of a divorce, the custody of living children would have stayed with the father, and there were no laws that protected the rights of the mother (Kapparis 233). However, if there was no living child and the woman switched under another man's guidance, would it have been possible for Antigenes to bring through any measure of punishment, or might this be why he accused her of homicide instead of abortion? In this regard, Todd argues that murder would have shifted the whole situation from a private to a public affair and justified the accusation in front of a jury (Todd 247). However, I suggest that there might be further reasons why the matter was discussed publicly.

Accordingly, scholar Nancy Demand raises the question of whether the risk for women to die by giving birth might have been an equal distribution to society than men who fell at war and found evidence that in Sparta, for instance, women who died in childbirth and men who died in a battle have been honored on tombstones likewise (253). I argue that even though there were no equal honors found in ancient Athens (Demand 261), it might be reasonable that the wife of Antigenes brought heavy shame over her oikos when she decided to induce an abortion that prompted her husband to file for divorce. This argument could be assured by the fact that it was common sense for women to bear children to deliver potential soldiers for the city (Brule 140). From this point of view, it might have been reasonable that Antigenes' wife refused to fulfill her duty to provide a potential son and soldier for the community and disgraced her oikos. Therefore, it is also likely that Antigenes made a public accusation of homicide instead of abortion.

Another motive for Antigene's accusation might have been the question of inheritance. In general, the birth of a son was not just higher appreciated in terms of military duties, but also from a financial aspect. However, there are critical elements here that, while linked, should be formally distinguished. Having a daughter would have meant a higher financial burden for the oikos such as the dowery for the future husband of the daughter (Brule 164) different than a son, who would not just protect the lineage of the family but would also be considered an heir to the father's oikos (Pepe 58). Keeping the above financial aspects in mind, it might be comprehensible why Antigenes filed for homicide along with the prevention from fatherhood. As the 5th fragment describes the aborted fetus "was fleshy, with the major organs already shaped, about four fingers long, but without bones, and then round and thick" (Hipokr. frg. 2,2,19). Unfortunately, the part with the official statement of the doctors and midwives is not sustained, however as we know from today, the above description would have made it possible to at least identify the sex of the fetus. I doubt that Antigenes would have accused his wife of homicide if she aborted a girl due to the above reasons, however likely is that he felt betrayed by a son and therefore filed publicly for homicide.

In this regard, and due to the reference to a similar case in the 4th fragment discussing whether the fetus might have been considered a human being, it is arguable that the medical experts involved in the case might have confirmed this assumption (Lys. fr. 20a). I follow from what I demonstrated above and argue that first, we already learned from Aristotle's argumentation that abortion was only acceptable as long as the fetus did not develop organs, which was apparently the case. Secondly, ancient Athenians believed that it was already possible to identify the male sex of a fetus forty days after conception (Brule 87). Therefore, it was very likely that the fetus was considered human, and homicide from this perspective might have been plausible. Unfortunately, we do not know the age of the mother and whether she felt obliged to abort because she was over the recommended age limit of Plato and feared health risks or death at birth.

Considering Kapparis' previous description of this case as "extraordinary and truly intriguing" (23), I agree that the incomplete transmission will not shed further light on the various questions that remain regarding the outcome of the case, as well as the related legal situation of the woman in charge. However, as the above fragments are in all likelihood part of a court speech, and the accusation of homicide was seemingly a public legal affair, there had been certainly a verdict for the woman, which is unfortunately not transmitted. The same goes for the part in which the medicines confirmed the legal status of the aborted child and with it confirmed the justification of homicide, which would have had a tremendous influence on the outcome of the case. Likewise, we don't know more about the exact legal relations between Antigenes and his wife, nor his motives to sue her publicly or her motives to abort the child or other possible circumstances that might have caused a miscarriage.

Nevertheless, what we do know from the above facts is that I could prove the existence of a legal sphere for this particular woman before the court, though, restricted because she was not able to speak up for herself but through the representation of her closest male relative. As I showed in the previous chapter, this was a common social convention of that time and not by all means to suppress the female. According to whether her advocate had highly evaluated skills in rhetoric, this could have influenced the outcome of the verdict either in a positive, or negative way.

Further, I proved that from a legal perspective, there was at least no law that explicitly prohibited abortion for women, likewise, medicines had not to fear legal punishment if they decided to act against the Hippocratic Oath and provide medical help to induce abortions. Even from a moral point of view, certain circumstances allowed women to end their pregnancies, which might answer the question in the 2nd fragment that women could seemingly not be punished for abortion by the state (Lys. fr. 20d). In contradiction, there are certain doubts about whether the absence of such legislation was to guarantee this right to women or because it was obviously the sole right of men. As discussed above, most arguments invalidate the first assumption.

CONCLUSION

A central contention of this research paper was to find evidence for the legal sphere of women within ancient Athens's society. Despite the above analysis proved certain democratic fields within Athens's law system according to its time, for instance as the female population had the right to make claims or participate in trials, it's hard to avoid the conclusion that gender relations were just and equal, however, apparently due to social customs rather than exclusion. In essence, certainly, the legislation of the time did not generally intend to suppress women as earlier interpretations demonstrated, but there was in fact legislation such as inheritance that remain controversial and favored male interests.

Amid all this, it is proved that women had to face judiciary consequences in similarly to men. Despite the fact it stays questionable how just verdicts for women had been if we consider females' exclusion from jury positions, which might have affected more favorable outcomes for cases involving women, especially when it came to an emotional case such as the above-discussed matter concerning abortion.

Toward the end, there is certainly open space for the revision of previous research that predominately focused on the display of social and legal spheres of the male society. In a similar vein, there is room in other research fields to investigate an accurate picture of women within ancient societies and to shed light on a more accurate picture of the spheres of women in antiquity.

Works Cited

Primary source

Carey, Christopher, *"Lysiae Orationes com fragmentis"*, Oxford, 2007.

Secondary literature

Brulé, Pierre. *Women of Ancient Greece.* Edinburgh University Press, 2022.

Burkhard, Leonhard, et al. "Einleitung: Grosse Prozesse im Antiken Athen." *Grosse Prozesse Im Antiken Athen,* C. H. Beck Verlag, Munich, 2000, pp. 7-8.

Burkhardt, Leonhard. "Das Volk Als Richter: Politische Prozesse in Athen Im 4. Jahrhundert v. Chr." *Grosse Prozesse Der Römischen Antike*, Verlag C.H. Beck, Munich, 2012, pp. 161–173.

Deman, Nancy. "The Attitudes of the Polis to Childbirth: Putting Women into the Grid." *Sex and Difference in Ancient Greece and Rome,* Edinburgh University Press, 2003.

Kapparis, Konstantinos. *Women in the Law Courts of Classical Athens.* Edinburgh University Press, 2021.

Katz, Marilyn. "Ideology and 'The status of Women' in Ancient Greece" *Sex and Difference in Ancient Greece and Rome,* Edinburgh University Press, 2003.

Kitto, H. D. F. "The Athenian Woman" *Sex and Difference in Ancient Greece and Rome,* Edinburgh University Press, 2003.

Korkouta, Lambrini, et al. "Views of Ancient People on Abortion." *Health Science Journal,* vol. 7, no. 1, 2013. Accessed 23 Jan. 2023.

Pepe, Laura. "Abortion in Ancient Greece." www.Semanticscholar.Org, Accessed on 26 Aug. 2013, www.semanticscholar.org/paper/Abortion-in-ancient-Greece-Pepe/d71406aae24fbc302b14090398fdbbccb8c0b394. Accessed 23 Jan. 2023.

Rhodes, P. J., et al. *Athenian Democracy.* R. Oldenbourg Verlag München, 2007.

Schmitz, Winfried. "Haus und Familie im antiken Griechenland." *Enzyklopädie der griechisch-römischen Antike,* Edinburgh University Press, 2003.

Schnurr-Redford, Christine. *Frauen Im Klassischen Athen.* Akad.-Verl, 1996.

Thür, Gerhard, et al. "Das Gerichtswesen Athens Im 4. Jahrhundert v. Chr." *Große Prozesse Im Antiken Athen*, C. H. Beck Verlag, Munich, 2000, pp. 30–50.

Todd, S. C. "Lysias on Abortion." *Symposion 1999*, 14th ed., Böhlau Verlag Köln, 1999, pp. 235-255.